THE AMAZING PROPHECIES OF MUHAMMAD IN THE BIBLE

TWENTY-EIGHT PROOFS FROM THE BIBLE OF MUHAMMAD'S PROPHETHOOD

THE CLEAR RELIGION SERIES - **PART 5**

EXCERPTED FROM (WHO DESERVES TO BE WORSHIPPED?)

NO DOUBT THIS LIFE IS AN EXAMINATION
WHICH NEEDS YOUR FULL CONSIDERATION
AS TO WHAT YOU WILL TAKE TO
YOUR FINAL DESTINATION?
ONLY TRUE BELIEF AND GOOD DEEDS ARE
YOUR WAY TO SALVATION
(Muhammad Sherif)

MAJED S. AL-RASSI

EDITED BY ANN RONAYNE

REVISED 2018

مركز أصول
Osoul Center
www.osoulcenter.com

THE CLEAR RELIGION SERIES

King Fahd National Library Cataloging-in-Publication Data

Al-Rassi, Majed Bin Suleiman
The Clear Religion Series part 5: The Amazing Prophecies Of Muhammad in the Bible . / Al-Rassi, Majed Bin Suleiman .- Riyadh , 2021

76p ; 12 x 16.5 cm

ISBN: 978-81-19946-43-3

1-Islam	I- Tile
210 dc	1442/7827

L.D. no. 1442/78227
ISBN: 978-81-19946-43-3
LI.

مركز أصول
Osoul Center

+966 11 445 4900
+966 11 497 0126
P.O.Box 29465, Riyadh 11457
osoul@rabwah.sa
www.osoulcenter.com

CONTENTS

HONORIFIC PHRASES IN THIS BOOK

(the Exalted): used after the mention of God/Allah to express: *Glorified and Exalted is He*

(bpuh): *Blessings and peace be upon him;* used after mention of the Prophet Muhammad

(pbuh): *Peace be upon him;* used after mention of any prophet or after mention of Angel Gabriel

(May Allah be pleased with him): used after mention of a male Companion of the Prophet

(May Allah be pleased with her): used after mention of a female Companion of the Prophet

ABOUT THE WORD 'LORD'

The word lord in English has several related meanings. The original meaning is 'master' or 'ruler', and in this sense it is often used to refer to human beings: 'the lord of the mansion' or '*Lord* So-and-So' (in the United Kingdom, for example). The word *Lord* with a capital L is used in the lexicon of Islam to refer to the One and Only God-Allah. In Islam, there is no ambiguity about the meaning of this word. While it is true that one may occasionally use the word *lord* (whether capitalized or not) to refer to a human being, in Islamic discourse the reference of this term is always clear from the context. Whereas for Christians, Hindus and other polytheists, the word *Lord* with a capital L may refer to Allah, to Jesus or to some imagined deity, for Muslims, there can be no plurality of meaning. Allah alone is the Lord, and the Lord is Allah-not Jesus, not Rama, not any other being.

ABOUT THE WORD 'ALLAH'

Although the English word 'God' has often been used interchangeably in this book with the word Allah, there is a difference. 'Allah' is the word in Arabic that is translated as 'God'. However, 'Allah' has a much more precise meaning than 'God'. 'Allah' is not merely an Arabic term for the word 'god'. Instead, the root word of the word 'Allah' is *ilah*, which means 'a god'. There are countless numbers of made-up 'gods', but only One True God worthy of worship, Whose name is Allah. The word 'Allah' literally means 'the worshipped', or 'the God'. Allah is, thus, the proper name for the **only Being that is worthy of worship in truth**, the True Creator of the universe. By saying 'Allah', Muslims are, in essence, negating every other entity which people wrongfully worship, while affirming worship to Him alone. The name 'Allah' is how God Almighty has referred to Himself in the Quran, and how Prophet Muhammad (blessings and peace be upon him) also referred to Him. Therefore, in this work, the term 'Allah' will often be used in reference to this One and Only God Who is worthy of worship.

INTRODUCTION

Every individual is born into a religious environment that is not necessarily in accordance with his or her choice; children are raised to follow the religion or ideology of their family, society, or culture. Even as new-born babies, they are assigned either the religion of their family or the ideology of the state; in some countries, the child's assigned religion is even recorded on the birth certificate. By the time individuals reach their teens, they have usually accepted the beliefs of their parents or their particular society. Since these beliefs have come to feel normal to them, they may give no thought to examining and possibly changing them.

However, individuals often encounter, or are exposed to, various beliefs and ideologies throughout the course of their lives, leading many to question long-held beliefs, traditions, or philosophical ideas. They begin to question the validity of their own beliefs. Seekers of truth often reach a point of confusion, especially upon realizing that the believers of every religion, sect, ideology, and philosophy claim to profess the one and only truth.

Amongst these beliefs is the one which Christians hold against Muhammad (bpuh), the Prophet of Islam, that he is not a true Messenger of God (Allah, the Exalted).

Simply and logically, this book sheds light on biblical proofs that Muhammad (bpuh) is a true prophet of Allah, whose prophethood was foretold by the prophet who preceded him: Jesus (pbuh).

Before we proceed, here is a reminder that when beginning

the search for the true religion, one should keep in mind the following four things:

Firstly, Allah has given us the ability and the intellect to discover the answer to this crucial question, which is also a life-changing decision: **What is the true religion?**

Secondly, Allah, the Most Compassionate, has not left us to go astray without any guidance. Indeed, He sent us prophets with scriptures to show us the right path.

Thirdly, we should always remember the underlying reason for this search: the everlasting life to come depends upon adopting the true religion in this life. This should be our ultimate motivation and a driving force to keep us searching until we are completely satisfied.[1]

Fourthly, we can only determine the true path and make a rational and correct decision if we willingly put aside all the emotions and prejudices which often blind us to reality.

With this short introduction, I leave you to peruse this book

Kind regards,

Majed S. Al-Rassi
Phone: 966 50 5906761
e-mail: majed.alrassi@gmail.com

1 The Bible, in its present form, confirms that seeking the truth is the main cause for salvation. In John 8:32, it has been stated, "and you will know the truth, and the truth will set you free." Muslims believe that the existing versions of the Bible contain elements of the original true message, although it has been altered significantly over time.

MUHAMMAD (BPUH) IN THE BIBLE[1]

Allah, the Most Kind and Wise, did not leave the followers of Jesus (pbuh) to disagree forever; He sent Prophet Muhammad (bpuh) to reveal the facts and resolve the perceived mysteries or points of great division. Those who believe in the Bible should know that it includes nearly thirty prophecies about the coming of Prophet Muhammad (bpuh) as a prophet for all people, and these ultimately prove the truth of the religion which he came with (namely, Islam).

Hence, if the Bible (or another scripture) contains apparent prophecies about the coming of Prophet Muhammad (bpuh), then there is nothing unusual or objectionable in referring to such prophecies.

Describing true believers amongst the followers of Moses and Jesus (peace be upon them), the Quran has stated:

{Those who follow the Messenger, the unlettered prophet,[2] whom they find written in what they have of the Torah and the Gospel, who enjoins upon them what is right and forbids them

---

1 This chapter was compiled from *Muhammad in the Bible* by Dr Jamal Badawi and *What the Bible Says about Muhammad* by Ahmed Deedat.

2 Prophet Muhammad (bpuh) was illiterate; he could neither read nor write. No human had ever taught him a word. The wisdom behind his unlettered status is to repel false accusations that the Quran was written or authored by Prophet Muhammad (bpuh) himself. It should be noted that there were no Arabic-language Bibles in existence in the 7th century CE, when Muhammad (bpuh) lived and preached. Indeed, Prophet Muhammad (bpuh) was educated through the Quran, which was revealed to him by His Creator and which contained things that no other human being could have known. Additionally, the Messenger of Allah (bpuh) was the best of humanity in every aspect of his character, including his intellectual skills.

what is wrong, and makes lawful for them the good things and prohibits for them the evil, and relieves them of their burden and the shackles which were upon them. So they who have believed in him, honoured him, supported him and followed the light which was sent down with him-it is those who will be the successful.} *(Quran 7: 157)*[1]

The original Bible given to Prophets Moses and Jesus (peace be upon them) contained a complete profile and clear prophecies of the coming of Prophet Muhammad (bpuh). Even in its present form(s), the Bible still contains many such prophecies. Quoting Prophet Jesus (pbuh), the Quran has stated: {And [mention] when Jesus, the son of Mary, said: O children of Israel, indeed I am the messenger of Allah to you confirming what came before me of the Torah and bringing good tidings of a messenger to come after me, whose name is Ahmad. But when he came to them with clear evidences, they said: This is obvious magic.} *(Quran 61: 6)*

---

1 The translations of the meanings of the Quranic verses in this book have been taken from Saheeh International, *The Quran: Arabic Text with Corresponding English Meanings*. Please note that any quotation in this book from the Quran is the translation that we feel has the closest meaning to its original Arabic. The translation is not the Quran itself.

THE MAIN ATTRIBUTES OF PROPHET MUHAMMAD'S PROFILE IN THE BIBLE

The main elements in Prophet Muhammad's profile, as depicted in the Bible, are the following eight:

1. His name
2. His characteristics
3. The location from which he was to emerge
4. The message to be revealed through him
5. The fulfilment of prophecies which he foretold
6. The time when he was to appear
7. The unique proof
8. The consistency between Muhammad's and Jesus' teachings

1. HIS NAME

Proof 1: Prophet Muhammad (bpuh) is mentioned by name in ten places in the Gospel of Barnabas.

Prophet Muhammad (bpuh) is mentioned by name in ten places in the Gospel of Barnabas, in Chapters 39, 41, 44, 54, 55, 97, 112, 136, 165, and 220.[1] Consider the following explicit quote from Chapter 165:

The disciples answered: O Master, who shall that man be of whom you speak, who shall come into the world? Jesus answered with joy of heart: He is Muhammad; Messenger of God, and when he comes into the world, even as the rain makes the earth to bear fruit when for a long time it has not rained, even so shall he be

1 The Gospel of Barnabas is not included in either the Protestant or Catholic Bible.

occasion of good works among men, through the abundant mercy which he shall bring. For he is a white cloud full of the mercy of God, which mercy God shall sprinkle upon the faithful like rain.

It is a fact that the Trinitarian church has done its utmost to obliterate **all** existing copies of the Gospel of Barnabas and to either hide it from the masses or to label it a forgery.

2. HIS CHARACTERISTICS

Moses (pbuh) reported that God told him:

I will raise up for them a prophet like you from among their brothers.[1] And I will put my words in his mouth, and he shall speak to them all that I command him. And whoever will not listen to my words that he shall speak in my name, I myself will require it of him. (Deuteronomy 18:18-19)

So the coming prophet will have three characteristics, which are discussed in further detail below:

- He will be like Moses (pbuh).
- He will descend from the Ishmaelites, the brothers of the Israelites.
- He will say what God instructs him to say (for God will put "words in his mouth").

Proof 2: Is like Moses (pbuh).

As explained in ***A Brief Illustrated Guide to Understanding Islam***: There were hardly any two prophets who were as similar as

1 When these words were spoken, they were addressed to the Israelites. The most notable 'brothers' of Israelites (Jews, the descendants of Abraham through his second son Isaac) are the Ishmaelites (Arabs, the descendants of Abraham through his first son Ishmael).

Prophets Moses and Muhammad (bpuh). Both were given a comprehensive law and code of life. Both encountered their enemies and were victorious in miraculous ways. Both were accepted as prophets and statesmen. Both migrated following conspiracies to assassinate them. Analogies between Moses and Muhammad overlook not only the above similarities, but other crucial ones as well. These include the natural birth, the family life, and the death of Moses and Muhammad (bpuh) but not that of Jesus. Moreover, Jesus was regarded by his followers as the Son of God and not exclusively as a prophet of God, as Moses and Muhammad (bpuh) were and as Muslims believe Jesus was. So, this prophecy refers to Muhammad (bpuh) and not to Jesus, because Muhammad (bpuh) is more like Moses than Jesus [is].[1]

Some people believe that this prophecy refers to Prophet Jesus (pbuh), but this cannot be true. The following eight points of comparison among Prophets Moses (pbuh), Muhammad (bpuh), and Jesus (pbuh) demonstrate that Prophet Jesus (pbuh) does not fit this particular prophecy. This comparison is self-evident; it clarifies the identity of the prophet who was to come after Moses (pbuh).

Birth

The birth of Jesus (pbuh) was miraculous. According to Christian and Muslim beliefs, he was miraculously born of the Virgin Mary.[2] However, both Moses (pbuh) and Muhammad

---

1 Ibrahim, *A Brief Illustrated Guide to Understanding Islam*, 34.

2 In the Gospel of Matthew 1:18:
When his mother Mary had been betrothed to Joseph [the carpenter], before they came together she was found to be with child from the Holy Spirit.
Luke tells us that when the good news of the birth of a holy son was announced to her:
Mary said to the angel, "How will this be, since I am a virgin?" And the

(bpuh) were born in the usual manner, as a result of the physical association of man and woman. Therefore, Jesus is not like Moses, but Muhammad (bpuh) is like Moses.

Parents

Moses had a father and a mother, and so did Muhammad (bpuh). Jesus, however, had only a mother and no human father. Therefore, Jesus is not like Moses, but Muhammad (bpuh) is.

Marital status

Both Moses (pbuh) and Muhammad (bpuh) got married and had children. There is no record of a marriage and offspring in the case of Jesus (pbuh). Therefore, Jesus is not like Moses, but Muhammad (bpuh) is.

Death

Both Moses (pbuh) and Muhammad (bpuh) died due to natural causes and were buried. The end of the mission of Jesus (pbuh) on Earth was unusual: being raised up to the heavens, according to Islamic belief, and being crucified, resurrected, and then raised up, according to Christian belief.[1] According to Christians, Jesus died for the sins of the world, but Moses did not have to die for the sins of the world. He and Muhammad (bpuh) died due to natural causes. Therefore, Jesus is not like Moses, but Muhammad (bpuh) is.

---

angel answered her, "The Holy Spirit will come upon you, and the power of the Most High will overshadow you;" (Luke 1:34-35)

The noble Quran confirms the miraculous birth of Jesus in noble and sublime terms. See al-Rassi, *Eleven Facts about Jesus and His Mother (Mary) in Islamic Teachings*. It should be noted that it is not necessary for Allah to plant a seed in any human or animal; he merely wills it, and it comes into being. This is the correct view of the conception and birth of Jesus.

1 This subject is discussed in al-Rassi, *Is Original Sin a Fact*?

Prophethood

Jesus was regarded by later Christians as the Son of God and not as a prophet of God (Allah), as Moses and Muhammad (bpuh) were. Therefore, Jesus is not like Moses, but Muhammad (bpuh) is.

Acceptance/rejection of prophethood

Moses and Muhammad (bpuh) initially met with resistance and scepticism, but they both were eventually accepted by their own people, during their lifetimes, as prophets and leaders. This was not the case with Jesus.

When Moses learned of a plot to kill him, he left Egypt and went to Madyan, where he was welcomed and reassured by Jethro. After returning to Egypt later, Moses led the Jews out of Egypt to escape Pharaoh and his soldiers. There is no doubt that the Jews caused endless trouble for Moses as they wandered in the wilderness-one significant lapse was their worship of the golden calf-but ultimately, the Jews, as a nation, acknowledged Moses as a Messenger of Allah who was sent to them.

The Arabs made Muhammad's life terribly difficult during the first ten years of his mission, and he suffered very badly at their hands. After thirteen years of preaching in Makkah, he left his hometown of Makkah upon learning of a plot to kill him. He went to Yathrib, later called Madinah, and before his death, the Arab nation in general acknowledged him as a Messenger of Allah (bpuh).

In contrast, the Christian Gospels clearly confirm that with the exception of a few followers, Jesus (pbuh) was rejected by his people (the Israelites) throughout his lifetime. According to the Bible, "He [Jesus] came to his own, and his own people did not receive him." (John 1:11) Even today, after 2,000 years, his own people-the Jews-on the whole still reject him. Thus, from this aspect, Jesus is not like Moses, but Muhammad (bpuh) is.

Confrontation of the enemy

Moses encountered his enemies (the Pharaoh's army), who sought to destroy him and his followers before they could escape to the Red Sea. Muhammad (bpuh) also encountered his enemies (the pagan Arabs), who sought in several battles to destroy him and his followers. No such encounter was reported in the case of Jesus. On the contrary, Jesus was reported to have commanded his disciple Simon Peter to put his sword back into its sheath when he attempted to defend Jesus at the time of his arrest. From this aspect as well, Jesus is not like Moses, but Muhammad (bpuh) is.

Moral and military victories

Moses' encounter with his enemies ended with a military and moral victory. His enemies drowned, and Moses and his followers were saved.

Muhammad's encounters with his enemies also ended with his final military and moral victory over them. He and his followers re-entered the city of Makkah, the centre of plotting against him. Impressed with his truthfulness and magnanimity, the great majority of his former enemies chose to become Muslims and his ardent supporters. Jesus' victory against his enemies was only a moral victory, which did not involve an immediate military victory over them. Therefore, Jesus is not like Moses, but Muhammad (bpuh) is.

	MOSES	MUHAMMAD	JESUS
Birth	normal	normal	miraculous
Parents	mother and father	mother and father	mother, no human father
Marital status	married, children	married, children	unmarried, no children
Death	normal, buried	normal, buried	ascended to heaven, will return to Earth
Prophethood (in the eyes of followers)	seen as a prophet	seen as a prophet	seen as the son of God
Accepted by those he was sent to?	yes	yes	mostly no
Confronted enemies?	yes	yes	no
Moral, military victories?	yes	yes	no

Table 1: Comparison of characteristics among Prophets Moses, Muhammad and Jesus (peace be upon them all).

Conclusion

Given these eight points of comparison among Moses (pbuh), Jesus (pbuh) and Muhammad (bpuh), the rational conclusion is that Muhammad (bpuh) is the prophet referred to in Deuteronomy 18:18, “like you (Moses).”

Proof 3: Descends from the Ishmaelites, the brothers of the Israelites.

The two prophets, Muhammad (bpuh) and Moses (pbuh), were descended from two brothers, Ishmael and Isaac, respectively. To elaborate, Abraham (pbuh) had two wives: Sarah and Hagar. Hagar bore Abraham his first son, Ishmael (pbuh),[1] and then Sarah bore him Isaac (pbuh).[2] Ishmael became the grandfather of the Arab nation, and Isaac became the grandfather of the Jewish nation. The prophet who was foretold was to come not from the Jews (the Israelites) but from their brethren, the Ishmaelites. Prophet Muhammad (bpuh) is a descendant of Ishmael; hence he is that prophet.

Isaiah 42 refers to the 'servant' of God (42:1), His 'chosen' (42:1), and His 'messenger' (42:19). Isaiah 42:11 mentions that the 'chosen' one was from the descendants of Kedar. Who was Kedar?

These are the names of the sons of Ishmael, named in the order of their birth: Nebaioth, the firstborn of Ishmael; and Kedar, Adbeel, Mibsam. (Genesis 25:13)

So Kedar was the second son of Ishmael, and Islamic teachings tell us that they both were ancestors of Prophet Muhammad (bpuh).[3]

---

1 See Genesis 16:15.

2 See Genesis 21:2-3.

3 Isaiah 42:1-8 reads:
Behold my servant, whom I uphold, my chosen, in whom my soul delights; I have put my Spirit upon him; he will bring forth justice to the nations. He will not cry aloud or lift up his voice, or make it heard in the street; a bruised reed he will not break, and a faintly burning wick he will not quench; he will faithfully bring forth justice. He will not grow faint or be discouraged till he has established justice in the earth; and the coastlands wait for his law. Thus says God, the LORD, who created the heavens and stretched them out, who

Isaiah 42 prophesies the 'chosen' one (Isaiah 42:1), whose mission of prophethood would be for all the nations; this fits only Prophet Muhammad (bpuh), whose mission was for all nations, unlike the Hebrew prophets, whose missions were limited to Israel:

...he will faithfully bring forth justice. He will not grow faint or be discouraged till he has established justice in the earth; and the coastlands wait for his law. (Isaiah 42:3-4)

Let the desert and its cities lift up their voice, the villages that Kedar inhabits; (Isaiah 42:11)

Proof 4: Says what God instructs him to say.

Allah, the Almighty, put His words into the mouth of Muhammad (bpuh) by sending the angel Gabriel (pbuh) to convey the exact words he should repeat to the people. The words were not his own, since they did not come from his own thoughts. To clarify, when teaching a language, if the teacher asks a student to read or repeat after him, is he not putting foreign words into the student's mouth?

The words of the noble Quran were revealed in an identical manner.

History tells us that Muhammad (bpuh) was forty years of age at that time. One night during the month of Ramadan, he was in a

---

spread out the earth and what comes from it, who gives breath to the people on it and spirit to those who walk in it: "I am the LORD; I have called you in righteousness; I will take you by the hand and keep you; I will give you as a covenant for the people, a light for the nations, to open the eyes that are blind, to bring out the prisoners from the dungeon, from the prison those who sit in darkness. I am the LORD; that is my name; my glory I give to no other, nor my praise to carved idols.

cave some three miles north of the city of Makkah. In the cave, the archangel Gabriel (pbuh) commanded him in his mother tongue: *Iqra* (which may be translated as: read, proclaim, or recite)!

Muhammad (bpuh) was terrified; in his bewilderment, he replied that he was illiterate. The angel commanded him a second time, with the same result. For the third time, the angel uttered the same command. This time, Muhammad (bpuh) grasped that what was required from him was to repeat and to recite, so he repeated the words as they were put into his mouth:

{Recite in the name of your Lord Who created-created humankind from a clinging substance. Recite, and your Lord is the most Generous-Who taught by the pen-taught humankind that which it knew not.} *(Quran 96: 1-5)*

As soon as the awe-inspiring angel departed, Muhammad (bpuh) rushed back home, shaking in fear and sweating all over. He asked his beloved wife, Khadeejah (may Allah be pleased with her), to cover him up. He lay down, and she remained by him, calming him down and comforting him. When he had regained his composure, he described to her what he had seen and heard. She assured him that Allah, the Exalted, would not allow anything terrible to happen to him. During the next twenty-three years of his life, after being given the prophethood, words were 'put into his mouth' in the same way, and he uttered them. These words (verses) made an indelible impression on his heart and mind, and as the volumes of the sacred scripture (the noble Quran) grew, they were recorded on palm leaves, on animal skins, and on the shoulder-blades of dead animals-as well as in the hearts of his devoted disciples.

The words (revelation) were actually put into his mouth exactly as foretold in the prophecy under discussion, "I will put my words in his mouth." (Deut. 18:18) In a similar quote, Jesus (pbuh) says of the 'Paraclete' who will come after him:

When the Spirit of truth comes, he will guide you into all the truth, for he will not speak on his own authority, but whatever he hears he will speak. (John 16:13)

As a scholar of comparative religions has said:

Neither the content of the revelation, nor its form, were of Muhammad's devising. Both were given by the angel, and Muhammad's task was only to repeat what he heard.[1]

Proof 5: Unlettered prophet.

Muhammad's experience in the cave of Hira (later known as *Jabal an-Noor*, the Mountain of Light) and his response to that first revelation are the exact fulfilment of another Biblical prophecy. In Isaiah 29:12, we read, "And when they give the book to one who cannot read, saying, 'Read this,' he says, 'I cannot read.'"

It is a well-known fact that Prophet Muhammad (bpuh) could not read or write.[2] He was described in the Quran as the unlettered prophet.[3] Allah has also said:

{Nor does he speak from [his own] inclination. It is not but a revelation revealed, taught to him by one intense in strength.} *(Quran 53: 3-5)*

---

1 Parrinder, *World Religions*, 472.

2 The wisdom behind this has been discussed in an earlier footnote.

3 {Those who follow the Messenger, **the unlettered prophet**, whom they find written in what they have of the Torah and the Gospel... So believe in Allah and His Messenger, **the unlettered prophet**, who believes in Allah and His words, and follow him that you may be guided.} *(Quran 7: 157-158)*

Proof 6: Stammering lips.

The Book of Isaiah explicitly mentions, "For with stammering lips and another tongue will he speak to this people." (Isaiah 28:11, KJV) This verse correctly describes the 'stammering lips' of Prophet Muhammad (bpuh) reflecting the state of tension and concentration, as well as of unfamiliarity, that he experienced at the times when he was receiving revelation.

Proof 7: Revealed in sections.

A related fact is that the Quran was revealed in sections over a span of twenty-three years. It is interesting to compare this with Isaiah 28, which speaks of the same thing:

For it is precept upon precept, precept upon precept, line upon line, line upon line, here a little, there a little. (Isaiah 28:10)

Proof 8: Name of God.

Deuteronomy 18:19 reads, "And whoever will not listen to my words that he shall speak in my name, I myself will require it of him." This prophecy in Deuteronomy mentions that this prophet will speak the words of God, starting with the **name of God**. If we look at the Quran, we will find that every chapter except Chapter 9 is preceded by, or begins with, the phrase "In the name of God (Allah), Most Gracious, Most Merciful."

The very first passage of the Quran that was revealed to Prophet Muhammad (bpuh) reads:

{Recite in the name of your Lord Who created.} *(Quran 96: 1)*

Furthermore, Islam teaches people to start almost every action in their daily lives with the words, "In the name of Allah, Most Gracious, Most Merciful," and this is in accordance with the teachings of Prophet Muhammad (bpuh).

As mentioned earlier, the name 'Allah' is how Allah refers to Himself in the Quran and how Prophet Muhammad (bpuh) always referred to Him. To say, "In the name of Allah" is a far clearer fulfilment of the prophecy "he shall speak in my name" than are other common expressions such as "In the name of God" or "In the name of the Father."[1]

Other Biblical Characteristics Of Prophet Muhammad (Bpuh)

An equally interesting and most revealing profile of Prophet Muhammad (bpuh) can be found in the 42nd chapter of the Book of Isaiah. Let us examine some of the characteristics found there:

Proof 9: The "one in whom God's soul delights" is called the 'servant' of God (42:1, 19), His 'messenger' (42:19) and His 'chosen' (42:1).

Translated into Arabic, these titles read: *Abduhu, rasooluhu,* and *al-mustafa*. All the prophets were indeed slaves and elects of Allah, yet no prophet in history has been universally called by these specific titles, as Muhammad (bpuh) has been. The testimony of faith by which a person enters into the fold of Islam reads, "I bear witness that there is no deity worthy of worship except Allah, and I bear witness that Muhammad is His slave and messenger."

Virtually the same formula is repeated five times a day during the call to prayers, five times a day immediately before the beginning of prayers, nine times a day during the minimum mandatory prayers, and several more times if the Muslim

1 Referring to Allah (God) as 'the Father' is an example of the serious distortions in the Bible. Allah has said about Himself:
{He neither begets nor is born, nor is there to Him any equivalent.} *(Quran 112: 3-4)*

performs additional recommended prayers. The most common title used for Prophet Muhammad (bpuh), from the beginning of his mission until today, is *Rasool Allah* (the Messenger of Allah [bpuh]). The Quran has given him this title, and during his lifetime, he was addressed as such by his followers. The voluminous collections of hadiths have been narrated typically in these forms: "I heard the Messenger of Allah (bpuh) say..." or "The Messenger of Allah (bpuh) said..." He has been described in the Quran as "Allah's slave" and "Allah's Messenger."

Proof 10: He will not grow faint or be discouraged until "he has established justice in the earth" (42:4), "he shows himself mighty against his foes" (42:13), and he "bring[s] forth justice to the nations" (42:1).

While comparing the lives and missions of Jesus (pbuh) and Muhammad (bpuh), it is clear that this verse talks about Prophet Muhammad (bpuh). On more than one occasion, Jesus expressed how disappointed he was to be rejected by the Israelites. Also, Jesus was not present long enough to prevail over his enemies (beyond the moral victory, which is common to all prophets).

On the other hand, we find no trace of Prophet Muhammad (bpuh) being discouraged, even in the most critical moments of his mission. In the space of one year, his beloved and supportive wife, Khadeejah (May Allah be pleased with her) died after twenty-five years of successful marriage; his uncle Abu Talib, who was instrumental in protecting him from the fury of the pagan Arabs (in Makkah) also died. These two tragedies were combined with the fact that his followers constituted only a small persecuted and tortured group. Under such trying circumstances, Muhammad (bpuh) went to the city of Taif to invite people to Islam and to seek their support in his struggle against paganism. He was rejected, mocked, and stoned until his knees and feet bled. In spite of all this, he was never "discouraged" (to use the term from Isaiah 42:4).

When the angel of mountains offered him the chance to retaliate by destroying their city, he refused, in the hope that some of the descendants of these wicked people would worship Allah, and indeed, they did!

After this bitter struggle, Muhammad (bpuh) "prevailed against his enemies," establishing a strong community of believers who indeed brought "justice to the nations,"[1] especially in the Persian and Byzantine Empires. Many members of those nations were guided to Islam, while others suffered defeats. As such, he was truly "a light for the nations" and for the whole world as well.[2]

Proof 11: "He will not cry aloud or lift up his voice, or make it heard in the street;" (42:2).

From the life history of Prophet Muhammad (bpuh), it is known that he was described by these characteristics. Also, the Quran teaches these characteristics, saying:

{And be moderate in your pace and lower your voice; indeed, the most disagreeable of sounds is the voice of donkeys.} *(Quran 31: 19)*

Proof 12: "The coastlands wait for his law" (42:4).

The only prophet who came after this prophecy (made in Isaiah's time) with a complete and comprehensive code of law was Prophet Muhammad (bpuh). The law that was revealed to

1 See Isaiah 42:1.
2 See Isaiah 49:6.

him spread to all corners of the earth, even to the remote islands and the farthest deserts. Jesus did not bring a new law, but Muhammad (bpuh) did.

Proof 13: "My [God's] glory I give to no other" (42:8).

The greatest glory a person receives from God (Allah) is to be entrusted as His messenger to humankind and receive His glorious revelation. Not only did this apply to Prophet Muhammad (bpuh), but it applied to him uniquely as the last and final messenger and prophet of Allah. Truly, Allah's glory (revelation of scriptures) was not given, and will not be given, to any other prophet after Muhammad (bpuh); he is the 'seal' of all prophets. After a letter or a message has been written, folded and sealed, nothing further can be added to it. It has been more than 1400 years since Muhammad (bpuh) was sent and the Quran was revealed to him. Yet we hear of no genuine prophet having the magnitude and influence on humanity to be compared with such figures as Abraham (pbuh), Moses (pbuh), Jesus (pbuh), and Muhammad (bpuh); nor do we hear about another post-Quranic glory or holy book that has influenced humankind to such an extent.

Proof 14: A descendant of Ishmael (pbuh).

The person to come was connected with the Arabs, specifically with the descendants of Ishmael (pbuh) who settled in Makkah and its environs. Isaiah 42:11 leaves absolutely no doubt about the identity of that prophet.

Let the desert and its cities lift up their voice, the villages that Kedar inhabits; let the habitants of Sela [the rock] sing for joy, let them shout from the top of the mountains.

According to the Book of Genesis (25:13), Kedar was the

second son of Ishmael. The best of the prophets from Ishmael's descendants is Muhammad (bpuh). His enemies (of his own clan), who were misled by their leaders, or "mighty men" (as described in Isaiah 21:17), ultimately embraced Islam and were embraced by it. Indeed, they had reason to "lift up their voice," to "sing" praise of God, and to "shout from the top of the mountains."

This "shouting" is chanted annually, by multitudes of Muslims from all over the world, from Mount Arafah and other places as part of the annual rites of Hajj (pilgrimage):
Here I am [at Your command], O Allah. Here I am. Here I am. There is no partner with you [in our worship]. Here I am at Your command. Verily, yours is the praise, the blessings and sovereignty. There is no partner besides you [in our worship].

Proof 15: He will be sent "to open the eyes that are blind, to bring out the prisoners from the dungeon, from the prison those who sit in darkness." (42:7)

Many of those who were opposed to the truth, and who fought Muhammad (bpuh) bitterly, nevertheless ended up as the most devout believers, with their blindness to the truth cured. Those who lived in the darkness of an unholy life came to the light of truth through the mission of Muhammad (bpuh).

No wonder the Quran describes itself as light manifest. Describing the Quran, Allah has addressed Prophet Muhammad (bpuh):

{...[This is] a book which We have revealed to you [O Muhammad], that you might bring humankind out of darknesses into the light by permission of their Lord-to the path of the Exalted in Might, the Praiseworthy.} *(Quran 14: 1)*

Proof 16: "Sing to the Lord a new song, his praise from the end of the earth..." (42:10)

Another indication (other than the prophecy in Deuteronomy) is that Isaiah ties the messenger connected with Kedar to "a new song" to be sung to the Lord. (Isaiah 42:10-11) This new song may refer to a new scripture in a language other than the language of the Israelite scriptures. This interpretation seems consistent with a more explicit mention of someone who will be speaking to people (including the Israelites) in "a foreign tongue." (Isaiah 28:11)

This explanation seems to fit closely with the verse that speaks of the praise of God "from the ends of the earth." (Isaiah 24:16) Only in the case of Islam do we find this prophecy realized in amazing accuracy. In all corners of the earth, five times every day, the praise of Allah and His last messenger, Muhammad (bpuh), is chanted from the minarets of hundreds of thousands, perhaps even millions, of mosques around the world. Praising Abraham and his descendants, along with Muhammad (bpuh) and his descendants, is a part of the five daily obligatory prayers; in addition, millions of devout Muslims praise Allah and Muhammad (bpuh) frequently throughout the day.

The 42nd chapter of Isaiah is indeed a fascinating one. It is not a casual or ambiguous reference to the Messenger of Allah (bpuh), who was to come centuries later. It is instead a comprehensive profile fitting only one person: Prophet Muhammad (bpuh). After all, the chapter relates this profile to Kedar, son of Ishmael, and no other descendant of Ishmael fits this description except Muhammad (bpuh).

Proof 17: Riding the camel.

Prophet Isaiah (pbuh) prophesied the coming of two leaders, whom he metaphorically called 'chariots', one riding a donkey and another riding a camel. "And he saw a chariot with **a couple of horsemen, a chariot of asses, and a chariot of camels**; and he hearkened diligently with much heed." (Isaiah 21:7, KJV)

Who are the "couple of horsemen"?

They are Jesus (pbuh) and Muhammad (bpuh). Let us examine the proof:

Jesus fulfilled the riding of the donkey prophecy, which says, "And Jesus found a young donkey and sat on it, just as it is written." (John 12:14)

The quote "just as it is written" is referring to Isaiah 21:7. It is important to know that nowhere in the New Testament do we see Jesus (pbuh) riding any camel. Nowhere in the New Testament do we see any fulfilment of any kind about the prophecy of riding the camel.

When we look at Muhammad (bpuh), he rode camels many times during his lifetime. Perhaps the most well-known incident is when he migrated from Makkah to Madinah to escape the torture of the pagans. When Muhammad (bpuh) rode into Madinah on his camel, the members of each group/tribe wanted him to be in their own neighbourhood. In order to avoid hurting anyone's feelings, the Prophet (bpuh) released the reins of his camel so that it could walk freely, and then he let it settle at the location chosen by Allah. This wisdom from Prophet Muhammad (bpuh) solved the problem.

Now, the open questions to any Jewish rabbi, or Christian priest or minister, are as follows:

- Where in the Bible do we see the fulfilment of the prophecy about riding the camel?
- In the Bible, who was the prophet who rode the camel, thus fulfilling the prophecy of Isaiah 21:7? The New Testament fulfils the riding of the donkey prophecy (of John 12:14), and it claims that it fulfilled only that prophecy. There is still an unfulfilled prophecy in the New Testament regarding riding the camel.
- If Prophet Muhammad (bpuh) was not the one who fulfilled the remainder of the prophecy in Isaiah 21:7, then who was that prophet?

These prophecies in the Old and New Testaments predict, in unequivocal terms, the coming of Prophet Muhammad (bpuh) and the genuineness of his prophethood.

3. THE LOCATION FROM WHICH HE WAS TO EMERGE

Proof 18: Deuteronomy 33:1-2.

Deuteronomy 33:1-2 combines references to Moses (pbuh), Jesus (pbuh), and Muhammad (bpuh). It speaks about God's revelation coming from Sinai, rising from Seir (probably the village of Sair near Jerusalem) and shining forth from Paran. According to Genesis 21:21, the wilderness of Paran was the place where Ishmael (pbuh) settled. In other words, it was in Arabia, and specifically in Makkah.

Another sign of the prophet to come from Paran (Makkah)

was that he would come with "ten thousands of holy ones." (Deuteronomy 33:2) That was the same number of faithful who accompanied Prophet Muhammad (bpuh) to Makkah in his victorious, bloodless return to his birthplace to destroy the remaining symbols of idolatry in the Kaaba. The text says, "he shone forth from Mount Paran; he came from the ten thousands of holy ones, with flaming fire[1] at his right hand."

According to Islamic history, the city of Makkah (Paran) was liberated by Prophet Muhammad's 10,000 troops.

If Muhammad (bpuh), who liberated the city of Paran with 10,000 believing men ("holy ones"), was not the one who fulfilled this Biblical prophecy and ended the worship of the 365 gods (in the form of idols), then who was that prophet? Is there another prophet who marched upon Makkah with this exact same number of men? The historical answer is: Prophet Muhammad (bpuh) is the only prophet whom this prophecy fits perfectly.

Proof 19: Habakkuk 3:3.

Habakkuk 3:3 speaks of God (God's help) coming from Teman (an oasis north of Madinah, according to Hastings' *Dictionary of the Bible*),[2] and the "Holy One" coming from Paran. That "Holy One" who, under persecution, migrated from Paran (Makkah) to be received enthusiastically in Madinah was none other than Prophet **Muhammad** (bpuh).

---

1 The meaning of the Hebrew word used here is uncertain.

2 Hastings, James, entry for 'Tema', *Hastings' Dictionary of the Bible*, accessed May 8, 2017, http://www.studylight.org/dictionaries/hdb/view.cgi?n=5416.

Indeed, the incident of the migration of the Prophet (bpuh) and his persecuted followers is vividly and prophetically described in **Isaiah 21:13-17**. That section foretold the battle of Badr as well, in which the few ill-armed faithful miraculously defeated the "mighty men" of Kedar, who sought to destroy Islam and intimidate their own folks who had turned to Islam. The text reads:

The oracle concerning Arabia. In the thickets in Arabia you will lodge, O caravans of Dedanites. To the thirsty bring water; meet the fugitive with bread, O inhabitants of the land of Tema. For they have fled from the swords, from the drawn sword, from the bent bow, and from the press of battle. For thus the Lord said to me, "Within a year, according to the years of a hired worker, all the glory of Kedar will come to an end. And the remainder of the archers of the mighty men of the sons of Kedar will be few, for the LORD, the God of Israel, has spoken." (Isaiah 21:13-17)

4. THE MESSAGE TO BE REVEALED THROUGH HIM

The Bible foretells the story of revelation.

Proof 20: Prophet Muhammad (bpuh) was illiterate.

Throughout his entire life, he never learned to read or write. The exact circumstances of the first revelation have been mentioned: it was the habit of Muhammad (bpuh) to frequently get away from the midst of his fellow Arabs and their heathen ways and spend many days secluded in the cave of Hira in the mountains of Makkah. There, he would pray to Allah, the Exalted, according to the practice of Abraham (pbuh). When he reached the age of forty (in 610 CE), the angel Gabriel (pbuh) appeared before him in that cave one day and ordered him to recite. Muhammad (bpuh), in his terror, thought he was being asked to read, so he stammered that he was unlettered. The angel Gabriel (pbuh) again ordered him to read, but Muhammad (bpuh) again informed him that he was unlettered. The angel Gabriel (pbuh) took hold of him firmly and commanded him, "Recite, in the name of your Lord, Who created!" Now Muhammad (bpuh) began to understand that he was not being asked to read, but to recite and to repeat. He began to repeat after him, and Gabriel (pbuh) revealed to him the first verses of the Quran that were revealed:

{Recite in the name of your Lord, Who created-created man from a clinging substance. Recite, and your Lord is the most Generous-Who taught by the pen-taught man that which he knew not.} *(Quran 96: 1-5)*

As mentioned earlier, the actual word used by angel Gabriel (pbuh) to address Muhammad (bpuh) was the Arabic word *iqra*, which means to read, recite, or rehearse. It is derived from the Arabic root word *qara*. However, if we were to go back to the original Hebrew form of the verses of Isaiah 29:11, we would find that the actual word which is translated into English as "Read this" is the Hebrew word *qara* [kaw-raw]. Is it just an amazing coincidence that the Hebrew text used not only a word with the same meaning, **but the exact same word itself**? Isaiah 29:11-18 reads:

11 And the vision of all this has become to you like the words of a book that is sealed. When men give it to one who can read, saying, "Read this," he says, "I cannot, for it is sealed."

12 And when they give the book to one who cannot read, saying,

"Read this," he says, "I cannot read."

13 And the Lord said: "Because this people draw near with their mouth and honor me with their lips, while their hearts are far from me, and their fear of me is a commandment taught by men,

14 therefore, behold, I will again do wonderful things with this people, with wonder upon wonder; and the wisdom of their wise men shall perish, and the discernment of their discerning men shall be hidden."

15 Ah, you who hide deep from the LORD your counsel, whose deeds are in the dark, and who say, "Who sees us? Who knows us?"

16 You turn things upside down! Shall the potter be regarded as the clay, that the thing made should say of its maker, "He did not make me"; or the thing formed say of him who formed it, "He has no understanding"?

17 Is it not yet a very little while until Lebanon shall be turned into a fruitful field, and the fruitful field shall be regarded as a forest?

18 In that day the deaf shall hear the words of a book, and out of their gloom and darkness the eyes of the blind shall see.

Remember that when a statement in the earlier scriptures is found also in the Quran, then this is proof of its validity. This is because if it is confirmed by the later scripture, it is clearly a remnant of the original revelation, which was not deleted or changed over time by those who rewrote the Bible.

5. FULFILMENT OF PROPHECIES WHICH HE FORETOLD

Proof 21: One may ask what criterion should be used to distinguish a genuine prophet from a false prophet (who might also presume to speak in the name of Allah)?

The answer to this question is clearly given in the concluding verses of Chapter 18 of the Book of Deuteronomy:

And if you say in your heart, 'How may we know the word that the LORD has not spoken?'-when a prophet speaks in the name of the LORD, if the word does not come to pass or come true, that is a word that the LORD has not spoken; the prophet has spoken it presumptuously. You need not be afraid of him. (Deuteronomy 18:21-22)

Jesus (pbuh) is reported to have said about his successor, "He will declare to you the things that are to come." (John 16:13)

It is a fact that not a single prophecy made by the Quran or by Prophet Muhammad (bpuh) has proved to be inaccurate in the least. Every prophecy made about the near future during his time did come to pass. Examples of these are:

- The prophecy that Muslims would conquer the two 'superpowers' of their time,[1] the Persian and Byzantine empires. This prophecy was made when Muslims were few and weak, when to prophesy their mere physical survival would have sounded too hopeful!
- Another prophecy was that Suraqah, a man who at one time was about to kill Prophet Muhammad (bpuh), would become a

1 Found in the chapter titled "The Romans" *(Quran 30: 2-5)*.

Muslim. Not only that he would become Muslim, but also that he would help the Muslim army conquer the Persian Empire and that he would have access to the Emperor's crown, which would be placed on his head! Not only did this prophecy appear to be a virtual impossibility when it was made, but it was as if the Prophet (bpuh) was looking distinctly at a scene that took place years after his death. The facts that Suraqah did become a Muslim and lived long enough to participate in the conquest of Persia, that the Muslims came out victorious, and that Suraqah had access to the Emperor's crown and actually wore it, can hardly be regarded as coincidence or a self-fulfilling prophecy.

Surely, it is no mere coincidence that so many of the prophecies that were described by the Prophet (bpuh) have actually happened, down to the last detail. (Some of the events that he foretold have not occurred yet.) Nor could such accuracy in each and every prophecy emanate from any individual other than a true and genuine prophet, according to the criterion stipulated in Deuteronomy 18:21-22.

Proof 22: Test of prophethood.

Jesus (pbuh) himself provided a sort of 'test', if you will, for those claiming prophethood:

You will recognize them by their fruits. Are grapes gathered from thornbushes, or figs from thistles? So, every healthy tree bears good fruit, but the diseased tree bears bad fruit... Thus you will recognize them by their fruits. (Matthew 7:16-20)

Anyone who applies this test to the teachings of Muhammad (bpuh) will find in the last testament of Allah-the noble Quran-the teachings which will bring to the world much-needed peace and happiness.[1]

"The ultimate criterion of a true prophet is the moral character of his teaching."[2]

George Bernard Shaw said of Muhammad (bpuh):

I believe that if a man like him were to assume the dictatorship of the modern world, he would succeed in solving its problems, and that would bring it the much needed peace and happiness.[3]

6. THE TIME WHEN HE WAS TO APPEAR

Proof 23: God's promise to make Ishmael (pbuh) a great nation.

It is well-known that from the descendants of Ishmael (pbuh) came the last great prophet of monotheism, Prophet Muhammad (bpuh), whose followers constitute a great nation that makes up nearly one-fifth of the total world population in all corners of the earth today.

"And I will make a nation of the son of the slave woman also, because he is your offspring." (Genesis 21:13)

Genesis 21:18 says about Ishmael (pbuh), "I will make him into a great nation."

In Matthew 21:19-21, Jesus (pbuh) cursed a fruitless fig tree (a biblical symbol of the prophets' heritage), which immediately withered and died. In a later verse in the same chapter, Jesus

1 See al-Rassi, *The Beautiful Teachings of Islam*.
2 Dummelow, *Commentary on the Holy Bible*.
3 Shaw, *The Genuine Islam*, 1:8.

(pbuh) said, "Therefore I tell you, the kingdom of God will be taken away from you and given to a people producing its fruits." (Matthew 21:43) That nation is made up of Ishmael's descendants (the rejected stone in Matthew 21:42).[1] It was victorious against all the superpowers of its time, as prophesied by Jesus (pbuh) when he said, "And the one who falls on this stone will be broken to pieces; and when it falls on anyone, it will crush him." (Matthew 21:44)

Moreover, in the Old Testament, Genesis 12:1-3, it can be found that God Almighty promised to create "a great nation" from Ishmael (pbuh), Abraham's first son and the forefather of the Muslims:

Now the LORD said to Abram [Abraham], "Go from your country and your kindred and your father's house to the land that I will show you. And I will make of you a great nation, and I will bless you and make your name great, so that you will be a blessing. I will bless those who bless you, and him who dishonors you I will curse, and in you all the families of the earth shall be blessed." (Genesis 12:1-3)

The quote "go... to the land that I will show you" is referring to the city of Paran (Makkah). The quote "I will make of you a great nation" is quite interesting; it describes perfectly the followers of Prophet Muhammad (bpuh), namely the Muslims.

As you probably know, Muslims worship Allah Almighty by prostrating to Him. Every time they pray and prostrate, they end their prayer by sitting on their knees and saying the following exact quote (translated from Arabic), "...and bless Prophet

---

1 "...The stone the builders rejected has become the cornerstone..." (Matthew 21:42)

Muhammad and the family of Prophet Muhammad, as You have blessed Prophet Abraham and the family of Prophet Abraham..."

As can be clearly seen, Muslims bless Prophet Abraham (pbuh) every single day of their lives when praying to Allah Almighty. They also say, "peace be upon him" or "peace and blessings be upon him" when they mention his name or any other prophet's name.

Yes, the Muslims are the "great nation" that Allah Almighty has talked about; they are blessed by Him because they worship none but Him, and they bless Abraham (pbuh) every day (no fewer than nine times) in their prayers.

Proof 24: According to the Gospel of John, the Jews were waiting for the fulfilment of three distinct prophecies.

The first was the coming of Christ. The second was the coming of Elijah. The third was **the coming of the prophet**. This is obvious from the three questions that were posed to John the Baptist.

And this is the testimony of John, when the Jews sent priests and Levites from Jerusalem to ask him, "Who are you?" He confessed, and did not deny, but confessed, "I am not the Christ." And they asked him, "What then? Are you Elijah?" He said, "I am not." "Are you the Prophet?" And he answered, "No." (John 1:19-21)

If one looks in a Bible with cross-references,[1] he or she will find, in the marginal notes where the words "the Prophet" occur in John 1:21, that these words refer to the prophecy of

1 Nowadays, we can do this easily online.

Deuteronomy 18:15 and 18:18 (about raising up a prophet from their brothers). It can be concluded from this that Muhammad (bpuh) is the prophet mentioned there, because he is the only prophet who came after Prophet Jesus (pbuh), and he is the one who is "like unto him." Furthermore, it is obvious that the Jews and John knew that "the Prophet" and the Christ were two different persons, since each was referred to by a separate question.

Proof 25: John 16:7

Jesus (pbuh) is reported to have said:

Nevertheless, I tell you the truth: it is to your advantage that I go away, for if I do not go away, the Helper will not come to you. **But if I go, I will send him to you.** (John 16:7)

Some Bible commentaries explain that the term 'Helper' (which is sometimes translated as 'Comforter' or 'Advocate') refers to the Holy Spirit. This would not make sense because-according to the Gospels-the Holy Spirit was already present in the world, prior to Jesus' birth as well as during his ministry. Luke 3:22 has mentioned that the Holy Spirit descended on Jesus (pbuh) in the shape of a dove. However, this verse (John 16:7) implies that the "Helper" is yet to come and cannot come until Jesus leaves the earth.

7. THE UNIQUE PROOF

Proof 26: One of the proofs that Muhammad (bpuh) was the prophet mentioned in the Bible is that the message he came with has reached across the East and the West, and his community now extends all over the world, something which would not have occurred if he had not been a prophet.

8. THE LACK OF WARNINGS FROM PREVIOUS PROPHETS

Proof 27: Had Muhammad (bpuh) not been the mentioned prophet, then the prophets who came before him, especially Moses (pbuh) and Jesus (pbuh), would have done two things: first, they would have mentioned whom they referred to exactly, and second, they would have warned their peoples vehemently about Muhammad (bpuh) – and we would have seen this in their scriptures. All the prophets warned about false prophets and cautioned their people about following them and being guided by them. For example, the previous prophets mentioned the Antichrist by name, and even Noah (pbuh), who was the first messenger, warned his people about him. However, none of the prophets warned about Muhammad (bpuh). In fact, quite the contrary; Jesus gave good tidings of Muhammad (bpuh), praised him, ordered people to follow him, and forbade them from opposing or disobeying him.

9. THE CONSISTENCY BETWEEN MUHAMMAD'S AND JESUS' TEACHINGS

Proof 28: One important proof that Muhammad (bpuh) is the prophet foretold in the Biblical references is the absolute consistency between the original (undistorted) teaching with which Jesus and other prophets were sent and those with which Muhammad (bpuh) came. To clarify, these are: calling to monotheism, glorifying Allah in His supreme attributes, believing in the Oneness of Allah in His essence, forbidding people from ascribing any of Allah's attributes to him, and many others.[1]

1 See al-Rassi, *Islam's Revival of Jesus' Teachings*.

This is not a surprise, because every prophet revived the basic beliefs that had been distorted over time after the departure of the preceding prophet. Islam, being the final message, revived the basic beliefs and practices of all the previous messages, including the message of Jesus (pbuh). It clarified it and removed the misconceptions which had become attached to the pure creed with which Jesus was sent, so that people would find it clear and straightforward to follow.

As the well-known scholar and commentator on the Quran, Abdur-Rahman ibn Nasir as-Sadi, wrote:

If Prophet Muhammad (bpuh) was not a true prophet, then his message would have contradicted the common message of Jesus and other prophets before him. Instead, it revived it and re-instated it.

It should now be clear that the Biblical prophecies speak of none other than Muhammad (bpuh). Many thanks to Allah, Who made the path clear for us. It is interesting to note that in the year 571 CE, Jesus' prophecy was fulfilled. Muhammad (bpuh) was born into a community of Ishmaelite Arabs who had become polytheists and idolaters; when he reached maturity and was given revelation, Prophet Muhammad (bpuh) started preaching his message of the worship of Allah alone.

In the year 632 CE, he died and left this world; however, his bright message will remain with people until the end of this world.

Being a true follower of Jesus (pbuh) must involve more than lip service, wherein one merely says that he or she follows or loves Jesus (pbuh) in order to attain paradise and be saved from hellfire, and that is it. True followers of Christ should accept his prophecy about Prophet Muhammad (bpuh) and follow his teachings of 'Islam', meaning complete and devoted submission to the One and Only God: Allah.

Note: Not only did Prophet Muhammad (bpuh) vouch for Jesus' and Moses' prophethood, but he also testified to the prophethood of all the true prophets who had been sent before him. He neither denied any of them nor fabricated anything about them. This was unlike what the reigning kings usually do against the kings who have reigned before them. Had Muhammad (bpuh) been a liar or a fabricator of his message (Islam), he would have not spoken of their truthfulness or praised them the way he actually did. He would have lied about them, as was the practice of the enemies of God's messengers throughout history!

Indeed, God Almighty has mentioned this very fact about Prophet Muhammad (bpuh) in the Quran:

{Rather, the Prophet has come with the truth and confirmed the [previous] messengers.} *(Quran 37: 37)*

THIS IS IT

In this book, you have been shown the right path, and Allah has given you the ability to distinguish right from wrong. He has also given you the freedom of choice as to whether or not to accept the message of Islam. If you accept His call, you will be warmly welcomed into paradise. If you reject it, you will end up with the biggest loss ever imagined: the loss of paradise and the guarantee of dwelling in hellfire for all eternity. Take a moment to comprehend what eternity really means. It is a very frightening realization.

To those who have been faithful Christians, you are warmly welcome to embrace Islam because:

- Jesus asked his followers to follow Muhammad (bpuh) whenever he appeared.
- When Jesus comes back before the end of this world, he will follow Muhammad (bpuh) and abide by his teachings.[1]

Yes, since Jesus called his true followers to follow it while he was on the earth, and he will follow Islam when he comes back, all faithful Christians should follow Islam as well.

To those who have been believing Jews, remember that Abraham and Moses surrendered themselves completely to their Lord, whether they called Him Elohenu, God, or Allah. All pride in ethnicity or ancestry is vain; what will matter in the end is your individual relationship with your Creator. This means total submission: Islam.

---

1 See al-Rassi, *Eleven Facts about Jesus and His Mother (Mary) in Islamic Teachings.*

To those of other faiths or those who, until now, did not feel that they had any faith at all, consider this message **now**, without any reluctance or hesitation, before it is too late-**before death overtakes you**. It could be soon. Who knows?

A WHISPER

Some people are not able to find the truth because of their blind commitment to their beliefs. Their tenacious adherence is usually not based on an intellectual understanding of the teachings but on powerful cultural and emotional influences. Because they were brought up in a particular family or society, they firmly cling to the beliefs of that group, believing that they are upholding the truth.

There are others who are convinced about the religion of Islam and are mentally ready to embrace it. However, when they contemplate the drastic changes it will bring to their lives, changes that might not please their families and communities, they hesitate, and even after taking the decision, they sometimes go back and change their minds later.

It is whispered in their ears that no matter how much money, prestige, status, and power an unbeliever may have possessed in this life, he or she will never have enough to buy entrance into paradise. In the hereafter, the poorest inhabitant of Earth who has testified to the truth of Islam will be far happier and more dignified than the richest person who did not accept the message of Islam.

Rejecting Allah's message is the biggest sin that one can commit. For this reason, while the soul is still in his or her body, the wise individual should take this opportunity; he or she is still alive to accept Allah's message before it is too late. The time for repentance is limited because once death arrives, it is no longer possible to obtain forgiveness.[1] Allah has mentioned:

1 Compiled from Caraballo, *My Great Love for Jesus Led Me to Islam*.

{[For such is the state of the disbelievers] until, when death comes to one of them, he says: My Lord, send me back that I might do righteousness in that which I left behind. No! It is only a word he is saying…}[1] *(Quran 23: 99-100)*

Religion is, without question, the most important aspect of a person's life, for it determines whether or not a person is rightly guided. It follows, therefore, that choosing the true faith is the most important personal decision one must make, and this decision needs to be based on clarity and total conviction. When it comes to matters of religion and creed, nothing must be left to chance because the one who is truly guided-as opposed to the one who is not-will surely find eternal happiness in the hereafter!

Having been presented with the previous proofs, we should use our intellect to analyse and reason. A crossroad has been reached, and Allah (Glorified is He) calls on all people to follow the clear, straight road and avoid all the murky, dubious ones. The right path has now become distinct from the wrong path, as Allah has mentioned:

{There shall be no compulsion in [acceptance of] the religion. The right course has become clear from the wrong. So whoever disbelieves in *taghoot*[2] and believes in Allah has grasped the most trustworthy handhold with no break in it. And Allah is Hearing and Knowing.} *(Quran 2: 256)*

It is my duty and responsibility, as a resident of this great planet, and as one who has submitted my free will to the law and

1 The unbelievers will ask for a 'second chance' when they see the angels ready to punish them, but it will be too late; they were given the time, the intellect and the guidance, but they neglected it for years until time ran out.

2 taghoot: idols; everything evil that is worshipped.

commandments of the Supreme Being, to urge all human beings to stay away from the worship of false deities-to stop putting their faith in statues, sphinxes, figures, amulets, talismans, horseshoes, and any other objects that have been manufactured by humans or created by God. After first repenting, a person should submit completely to the will of Allah, the Only God of the universe.

HOW TO BECOME A MUSLIM

Every religion has its own requirements for conversion.

Someone who wants to become Jewish must pledge all of the following:

1. To enter the 'eternal covenant' between God and the people of Israel and to become a Jew of his or her own free will;
2. To accept Judaism to the exclusion of all other religious faiths and practices, which means to deny the prophethood of Jesus and Muhammad (bpuh) and to deny the revelations that God sent to humankind through them;
3. An undivided loyalty to Judaism and to the Jewish people under all circumstances;
4. To commit to learning the Torah and other Jewish knowledge; and
5. To raise his or her children as Jews.

To be a Christian, one must:

1. Believe that God (Allah) has a partner, a mother, and a son;
2. Believe that every new-born baby is born sinful;
3. Believe that God became a man and descended to Earth to die for the sins of the people;
4. Deny the prophethood of Muhammad (bpuh) publicly; and
5. Deny that the Quran is a revelation from Allah, the Exalted.

However, to become a Muslim is simple. One must:

1. Bear witness that there is no deity worthy of worship except Allah (in other words, disown all false gods),

2. Bear witness that Muhammad (bpuh) is His messenger,
3. Believe in all the six articles of faith, and
4. Worship Allah as taught by Prophet Muhammad (bpuh).

Hence, becoming a Muslim is a simple and easy process. If anyone has a real desire to be a Muslim and has full belief that Islam is the true religion of God, all he or she needs to do is to pronounce the *shahadah*, the testimony of faith.[1] Pronunciation of this testimony with a sincere heart brings the person into the fold of Islam. It is the main gateway to Islam.

Prophet Muhammad (bpuh) said:

«Whoever testifies that there is no deity worthy of worship except Allah, Who has no partner; that Muhammad is His slave and messenger; that Jesus is the slave of Allah, His prophet, and His word[2] which He bestowed in Mary and a spirit created from Him; that paradise (heaven) is true; and that the hellfire is true- Allah will eventually admit him into paradise, according to his deeds.» (Recorded by Bukhari)

The first part of the testimony consists of the most important words of truth that Allah has ever revealed to His noble prophets, "There is no deity worthy of worship except Allah." He has stated:

{And We sent not before you any messenger except that We revealed to him that: There is no deity except Me, so worship Me.} *(Quran 21: 25)*

---

1 The words of the *shahadah* are: *Ash-hadu al-la ilahailla Allah, wa ash-hadu anna Muhammadan Abduhu wa Rasooluhu.* (I testify that there is no deity worthy of worship except Allah, and I testify that Muhammad is His slave and messenger.)

2 It means that Jesus was created when Allah said the word "Be"; when He said it, Jesus was created in the womb of his mother, Mary.

Bearing this testimony implies that all forms of worship-whether praying, fasting, supplicating, seeking refuge, or offering an animal as sacrifice-must be directed to Allah and to Him alone. Directing any form of worship to other than Allah (whether to an angel, a prophet, Jesus, Muhammad [bpuh], a saint, an idol, a statue, the sun, the moon, a tree, a cross, or anything else) contradicts the fundamental message not only of Islam but of all the prophets; it is an unforgivable sin in the hereafter, so one must repent before death.

The second part of the testimony means that Prophet Muhammad (bpuh) is the slave and the chosen messenger of Allah.[1] This implies that a true Muslim obeys and follows the commands of the Prophet (bpuh) as mentioned in the collections of his hadiths. One must believe in what he has said, practice his teachings, and avoid what he has forbidden because the hadiths were, in fact, revelations and inspiration conveyed to him by Allah.

As mentioned earlier, Prophet Muhammad (bpuh) was sent in order to implement the Quran in a practical way through his sayings, deeds, and legislation, as well as all other facets of his life. When his wife Aishah (may Allah be pleased with her) was asked about his character, she replied:

«His character was that of the Quran.» (Recorded by Muslim and Abu Dawood)

Hence, to truly adhere to the second part of the shahadah is to follow his example in all walks of life. Allah has mentioned: {Say [O Muhammad]: If you should love Allah, then follow me,

1 The meaning of worship is, simply, total submission and complete obedience to Allah's commandments in belief, intentions, statements, and actions. This is what is meant by 'slavery to Allah' in Islam.

[so] Allah will love you and forgive you your sins. And Allah is Forgiving and Merciful.} *(Quran 3: 31)*

A true Muslim must strive to mould his or her life and character to emulate the Prophet (bpuh), for he was a living example for human beings to follow. Allah has said to His Prophet (bpuh): {And indeed, you are of a great moral character.} *(Quran 68: 4)*

Allah has also said to all people: {There has certainly been for you in the Messenger of Allah an excellent pattern for anyone whose hope is in Allah and the Last Day and [who] remembers Allah often.} *(Quran 33: 21)*

When one enters the fold of Islam, all previous sins are forgiven; one starts a new life of piety and righteousness since he or she, in essence, has repented from the ways and beliefs of the previous life. One man told the Prophet (bpuh) that he would accept Islam only under the condition that Allah would forgive his sins; the Prophet (bpuh) asked him:

«Do you not know that accepting Islam destroys all sins that came before it?» (Recorded by Muslim)

As soon as a person accepts Islam, he or she is free of all previous sins. The person's record is wiped clean, as if he or she was born that very day. One should try as much as possible to keep his or her records clean and strive to do as many good deeds as possible; the more good deeds, the more he or she will be elevated in paradise.

It should be emphasized again that accepting Islam does not mean turning your back on the messages of previous prophets (peace be upon them all). Indeed, it is a fulfilment of those messages. Therefore, if you are a Jew or a Christian, accepting

Islam and following Prophet Muhammad (bpuh) is a fulfilment of the messages which Moses and Jesus (peace be upon them) brought, as has been clearly described and proven in this book.

On the other hand, rejecting Islam means turning your back not only on Prophet Muhammad (bpuh) but also on Prophets Moses and Jesus. Doing so is actually a clear violation of their messages, and it diminishes your hope of paradise in the hereafter.

It is now up to you to decide where your own future home will be. I wish you all the best!

BEST DECISION THEY EVER MADE

Islam is often called the fastest growing religion, and each person who embraces Islam has a unique story and unique reasons. Despite widespread misconceptions about women in Islam, a growing number of women are finding that Islam is the true religion and the best way of life. Ann Ronayne's story is below; she welcomes emails from readers and can be reached at ann.ronayne1@gmail.com.

"Me? Go live in Kuwait? No way!" That was my reaction when my manager tried to persuade me to take a position in Kuwait. But I was to learn that {...the command of Allah is a decree of predestiny that is ever fulfilled.} *(Quran 33: 38)*[1]

I was born and raised in suburban Washington, D.C. in a Catholic family, and I attended Catholic schools. In the 1960s, the Catholic Church made major changes in its teachings in an attempt to be more modern; it tried to focus more on positive aspects and de-emphasize what was considered negative: punishment, regulations, abstinence from certain foods at certain times, etc. (Even so, Catholics in the West routinely ignored many of the rules that still existed, such as the prohibitions on contraceptives.) The Mass, which had always been said in Latin, was said in English instead. The nuns who taught us replaced their habits (modest dress) with modern clothes. Our religion classes had never involved reading the Bible, but now, instead of focusing on religious beliefs, they involved discussion of social issues and singing a lot of contemporary folk songs, as did the new Masses. It seemed strange that so much of what

1 This translation is taken from Hammad, *The Gracious Quran.*

we had been taught as the truth was now completely changed. Still, when we prepared for our first Holy Communion, we were taught that the bread that the priest was putting in our mouths was the actual body of Jesus (which would bleed if we were to bite it). For these and many other reasons, I doubted my religion and rejected it from a young age.

My decision was only confirmed as I learned more. If the trinity was such an important concept, why hadn't Jesus explained that clearly (and repeated it over and over again)? If God wanted to forgive us, He could have done that without coming to Earth Himself and being crucified to atone for our sins. Was it Jesus the man or Jesus the God who died on the cross, and how can God – Who has no beginning or end – die? If God did send His son (who was also God?) down to Earth to guide us, why would He neglect to give us the message during his thirty-three years, so that the truth had to be discovered and given to us later by Paul, who never even met Jesus?! If Christianity were the true religion, why didn't Jesus himself live and teach it?

For many years, I considered myself an atheist or an agnostic, but I was never concerned with choosing a label. I thought it was enough that I tried to be a good person, and I felt that nonbelievers actually did more good works because they didn't depend on any supernatural being for help. I never felt that I was searching for answers about the purpose of life or about religious beliefs.

After the Gulf War, I was working as a computer consultant when my company was offered a position in Kuwait which was perfect for me. My initial reaction was that I had no desire to go and work in a place where I thought women were treated as second-class citizens; after all, I had the usual stereotypes about women in a place like Kuwait. The manager on location assured me that the working environment was professional and that there were many bright women in the organization, including those who would be my supervisor and manager. I was eventually persuaded to take the contract for one year, thinking that it would be an adventure.

I soon learned that all of the stereotypes I had brought with me were wrong.

My colleagues were always friendly and respectful, and it occurred to me that it was almost the only environment I'd ever worked in where I saw no evidence of sexual harassment-not even any off-colour jokes or racy calendars hanging in cubicles. (It was certainly different from the atmosphere I'd experienced in the US military.) The women working with me were university graduates and were not shy about speaking out, and most chose to wear Islamic dress. Advertisements did not use women's bodies to sell products.

I was impressed to see the bonds among families and members of the society in general. When one colleague lost his pay check, all of the men quickly pitched in until they had collected the same amount of money for him. People also gave generously to the needy, both locally and globally.

When someone's mother called and said she needed something, the person would leave work to take her to the doctor or get what she needed. If a man's uncle died, all the men attended the funeral prayer; if a woman's aunt died, all the women went to visit her to give their condolences. When someone married or had a baby or recovered from an operation, an extensive network of family members, friends and colleagues shared that experience. Hospital rooms were large and even furnished with sofas and chairs to accommodate all the visitors.

The attitude towards the elderly was different from what I was used to, since extended families lived together, with several generations in one house; the children who didn't live in the same house came to visit often, if not daily. Grandparents had children and grandchildren living with them and were not left to live and die alone, or sent to nursing homes (which don't even exist). Older women were highly respected; they did not feel the need to make themselves look young and beautiful in order to gain self-esteem. Taking care of one's elderly parents was seen as a blessing and an opportunity for doing good deeds, rather than a burden, and care of one's parents is emphasized in the moral system of Islam. (This is not to say that non-Muslims in the West don't care about their parents, but there are different priorities and expectations. There is usually more of an emphasis on nuclear families and independence, with the elderly themselves not wishing to be a burden on their families.) In general, dealing with difficult situations was seen as a test and not a cause for despair. Taking one's own life was rare and also forbidden because only Allah has that right.

When the month of Ramadan came around, I was amazed by the idea that one billion Muslims around the world were fasting together-abstaining from food and drink every day from long before sunrise until the sun set. I joined them in fasting the entire month, although I had no intention of becoming Muslim and didn't experience the spiritual recharge that I would feel later as a Muslim.

At the time, I knew little about Islam, and I'm embarrassed to say now that I considered it a backwards religion which would only appeal to the ignorant masses. As I slowly realized that the stereotypes I had brought with me were all wrong, I became curious about the religion. As I learned more, I discovered that Islam was the reason for the moral system I had witnessed, and that these positive social aspects had been part of Islamic societies throughout the centuries. Even small things that had struck me-such as greetings given among strangers when one entered an elevator or an office-had their basis in Islamic teachings.

I got a Quran translation and some other books and began reading. Over and over again, I was surprised at what I found-and perhaps more by what I didn't find. I found a belief system which was rational and uncluttered, and I didn't find the oppression of women or terrorism that I had expected. I was attracted by the emphasis on social justice and standing up against oppression.

Obviously, the key question about religion is deciding whether or not it is true. Since this decision must rely on faith to some extent, how can we really know? One factor is the credibility of the sources; in the case of Islam, the most important source is the Quran.

I was struck by its scientific accuracy, demonstrated by statements which describe scientific phenomena that were not discovered until recently. I learned that the Islamic world had made major contributions to scientific knowledge and was the seat of civilization and learning while Europe was in the Dark Ages. Logically, I knew that an illiterate seventh century Arab could not have written this book himself. I began to question my idea that there was no Creator-that the intricate systems that made up the universe and its life forms could have developed randomly or that we were born, lived, and died with no purpose.

I was impressed that the Quran had never been changed over the years, so that the Quran we read today (in its original Arabic) is exactly the same as that revealed to Muhammad (bpuh) and passed on to his followers 1400 years ago. All Muslims memorize parts of it, and there are millions of people around the world who have memorized it in its entirety, so even if every copy disappeared today from the face of the earth, it would be easily recorded again. I couldn't help but to contrast that with the Bible, a collection of books written by various people over time; different Christian sects do not even agree on which books are included, and in some cases, scholars do not even know who wrote the books. We do not have the original sources, and there are different versions of the later sources. There are many contradictions, and the New Testament actually rejects many of the teachings of the Old Testament.

I was surprised to find out that Islam had the same roots as Judaism and Christianity, and that Muslims believed in the same prophets, including Abraham, Moses, and Jesus (peace be upon them all).

I began to understand why Muslims loved Prophet Muhammad (bpuh) so much, and I wondered why I never knew anything about him... never even knew that he was a historical figure about whom so much was known, and whose gravesite is known and visited. Authentic narrations from those who were closest to him describe him as a modest, truthful man who stood up for justice and against oppression.

I used to walk along the beach at night, looking up at the moon and stars and reflecting on Allah's creation, as the Quran recommended. I became convinced that the Quran must have been a message from God, but it took me a while to actually accept Islam… yet it was so rational and simple in its essence: one God, one Creator of the universe and everything in it, Who offered us guidance to make the best of our lives in this life and the next. Obviously, there are more details, but this sums up the Islamic beliefs, and one who accepts this is essentially a Muslim.

The concept seemed so pure and logical, especially when compared to the concept of the trinity, which cannot be explained rationally. There are three Gods, but they are one God? Jesus is both fully divine and fully human, so that he is all powerful yet experiences hunger and thirst and other physical needs? Moreover, this uncomplicated main principle of Islam – that there is one God – is repeated over and over again in the Quran, in the sayings of Prophet Muhammad (bpuh), and in the prayers of ordinary Muslims. If the trinity were the true essence of God, wouldn't it have been clearly explained and mentioned over and over again?

In Islam, God is just; He does not hold any of us accountable for the sins of another, which we had nothing to do with. There is no concept of original sin or of a crucifixion required to redeem all of us from that original sin perpetrated by someone else.

Of course, there were aspects that made me reluctant to make such a momentous change in my life. For example, although I understood the purpose and the benefits of Islamic dress, I couldn't imagine wearing it myself until I attended a Ramadan dinner at an organization for English-speaking Muslim women and met dozens of Western women who had converted to Islam, and who felt proud to dress this way.

For all the reasons mentioned above, and under no pressure from anyone, I came to the conclusion that the Quran was the word of God, and that Islam was the true religion.

On the day that I decided I was ready to officially declare my Islamic faith, I asked a co-worker to help me do so officially. There is actually no requirement to say this publicly or to get any kind of certificate; the declaration of faith is simply a matter of testifying that there is no deity worthy of worship except Allah and that Muhammad (bpuh) is his Messenger. It was a very moving experience, since I was essentially starting life over again, with a clean slate. It was undoubtedly the best decision I've ever made.

When we returned to the office, I went back to my desk and resumed work. It didn't occur to me that this was anything but a personal decision, and no one even knew that I was considering it… but my friend informed everyone, and to my surprise, I received congratulations from well-wishers for the rest of the day. That evening, she invited me to her aunt's house, and with only a few hours' notice, her mother, sisters, aunts, and cousins (most of whom I'd never met before) had a party for me, complete with gifts of Qurans, prayer dresses, gold, etc. Over the next days and weeks, I received dozens of gifts from co-workers (some of whom I had never met), friends, and acquaintances. I was very blessed, for I know that others who embrace Islam sometimes encounter many hardships.

In my feminist years, we spoke of 'sisterhood', but this was my introduction to true sisterhood. Muslim women considered me their sister, simply for the sake of Allah (God). Over the years, I've met so many amazing Muslim women of all nationalities and classes and educational backgrounds, and in our gatherings, we often talk about how blessed we are and how different our lives are from what many people think. It's hard to describe the feeling of standing in prayer, shoulder to shoulder with so many different women, knowing that we are sisters in Islam whether or not we even know each other.

It took me several weeks to build up the courage to wear the hijab (Islamic headscarf), but I found it liberating in a way that I hadn't expected. I was worried when I travelled to the U.S. wearing the hijab soon after becoming Muslim, but I needn't have been. Everywhere I went, I was greeted by other Muslims with the Islamic greeting *Assalamu alaykum* (Peace be upon you). I felt welcomed as a part of the worldwide Muslim community, and the hijab was what made that possible; if I wasn't wearing it, other Muslims would not have recognized that I was also Muslim and would not have offered those greetings.

I don't mean to claim that the Muslim community is some sort of utopia. Certainly, there are problems, but the problems are not from Islam; on the contrary, they are due to ignorance and rejection of Islamic beliefs and practices. The reality is that Islam does not need a reformation; Muslims do.

OTHER MUSLIMS WHO WERE FORMERLY CHRISTIANS

There are many Christian women and men from all backgrounds who have embraced Islam. The following is just a small sample of well-known contemporary Muslims who sincerely studied Christianity before rejecting it in favour of Islam. They were chosen because their stories (as well as their books, articles, and videos) are easily accessible online in English.

Dr Jerald Dirks is an American former Methodist deacon (minister) with a Master's in Divinity from Harvard University and a PhD in Psychology from the University of Denver. The more he studied the Bible, the more he realized that he could not accept Christian teachings, and the more he dreaded going back to preaching what he knew was not true. When he took his questions to other ministers whom he respected, some of them admitted (behind closed doors) that they agreed with him, but they could not abandon their religion without breaking up their families and cutting off their livelihoods. Dr Dirks, along with his wife Debra, realized that Islam was the religion that actually followed the message brought by Jesus (pbuh) and other Prophets of God. Read more about them at http://www.jeralddirksanddebradirks.com.

Yusha (Joshua) Evans was attending a Bible College in the southern United States, learning to read the Bible in Hebrew and Greek and intending to become a Christian missionary or minister. After reading the Bible cover-to-cover six or seven times, he was left wondering at the inaccuracies and inconsistencies he noticed. He left Christianity and began searching for the truth, but no religion satisfied him until he found Islam. See more about him at https://yushaevans.com.

Aminah Assilmi (d. 2010, may Allah have mercy on her) was an American Baptist who found herself in a class with some Arab Muslims and decided to try to convert them to Christianity. When her attempts failed, she asked for a copy of their Quran so that she could read it and show them the error of their ways.

After one and a half years of research, she ended up embracing Islam instead.

Dr David Liepert is a Canadian anaesthesiologist who started studying Islam with the intention of showing his Muslim colleagues that they were wrong and that Christianity was the truth. He sought to prove this by studying the Bible and trying to answer his own questions... yet he couldn't find the evidence to support his beliefs. His story is narrated in *Choosing Faith: Rediscovering the Commonalities Between Christianity & Islam*, which is available online at http://www.choosingfaith.com/.

Idris Tawfiq (d. 2016, may Allah have mercy on him) was a British writer and broadcaster who touched the hearts of many. He had a degree in English Language and Literature and taught in both the UK and Egypt. He also had a degree in Sacred Theology from the Pontifical University of Saint Thomas Aquinas in Rome; before embracing Islam, Idris was a Roman Catholic priest.

BIBLIOGRAPHY

Badawi, Dr Jamal. *Muhammad in the Bible*. Halifax, Canada: Islamic Information Foundation (IIF).

Caraballo, Simon (Muhammad bin Abdullah Caraballo). *My Great Love for Jesus Led Me to Islam*. Jubail, KSA: Dawah & Guidance Centre.

Deedat, Ahmed. *What the Bible Says About Muhammad.*

Dummelow, John R. *Commentary on the Holy Bible.* UK: Macmillan Publishers Limited, 1970.

Ibrahim, I. A. *A Brief Illustrated Guide to Understanding Islam*. Houston, TX: Darussalam, 1997.

Liepert, David. Choosing Faith. Riyadh: International Islamic Publishing House, 2011. (Available online at http://www.choosingfaith.com/.)

Parrinder, Geoffrey. *World Religions: From Ancient History to the Present*. New York: Checkmark Books, 1985.

al-Rassi, Majed. *Eleven Facts about Jesus and His Mother (Mary) in the Islamic Teachings*. http://www.saaid.net/The-clear-religion/04.pdf.

__. *Is Original Sin a Fact?* http://www.saaid.net/The-clear-religion/030.pdf.

__. *Islam's Revival of Jesus' Teachings.* http://www.saaid.net/The-clear-religion/05.pdf.

__. *The Beautiful Teachings of Islam.* http://www.saaid.net/The-clear-religion/029.pdf.

__. *Who Deserves to Be Worshipped?* http://www.saaid.net/The-clear-religion/017.pdf.

Saheeh International. *The Quran: Arabic Text with Corresponding English Meanings.* Jeddah: Abul Qasim Publishing House, 1997.

Shaw, George Bernard. *The Genuine Islam*. Singapore, 1936.

APPENDIX

For Further Information about Islam

- Ata ur-Rahim, Muhammad and Ahmad Thomson. *Jesus: Prophet of Islam*. Riyadh: International Islamic Publishing House, 2008.
- Baagil, M. *Christian-Muslim Dialogue*. Riyadh: International Islamic Publishing House.
- Bucaille, Maurice. *The Quran and Modern Science*. Riyadh: International Islamic Publishing House, 2001.
- Khan, Maulana Wahiduddin. *God Arises*. Riyadh: International Islamic Publishing House, 2005.
- Khan, Abdul Waheed. *The Personality of Allah's Last Messenger*, 2nd ed. Riyadh: International Islamic Publishing House, 2007.
- LeBlanc, Abdul-Malik. *The Bible Led Me to Islam.* Toronto: Al-Attique Publisher.
- Philips, Dr Abu Ameenah Bilal. *The Purpose of Creation.* Riyadh: International Islamic Publishing House.
- Philips, Dr Abu Ameenah Bilal. *The True Message of Jesus Christ*. Riyadh: International Islamic Publishing House, 2006.
- al-Uthaymeen, Shaykh Muhammad ibn Saalih. *Explanation of the Three Fundamental Principles of Islaam.* UK: Al-Hidaayah Publishing and Distribution, 1997.

Online Information about Islam

- islam-guide.com
- iera.org

- islamtomorrow.com
- discoveritsbeauty.com
- edialogue.org (live chat)
- islamhouse.com/en/ (thousands of free books)
- iera.org/shop/ (free downloads)
- iiph.com

GLOSSARY OF ISLAMIC TERMS[1]

abu (or *abi*)	father (of)
Allahu akbar	Allah is the Greatest
Arafah (or Arafat)	the plain outside of Makkah where pilgrims gather at the climax of the Hajj; Mount Arafah falls inside that plain. It is the mountain beside which Prophet Muhammad (bpuh) stood when he made his Hajj.
hadith	a statement or action of Prophet Muhammad (bpuh) that was remembered and recorded by his Companions and followers
Hajj	the major pilgrimage to the Sacred Mosque, site of the Kaaba in Makkah, to be undertaken by every able Muslim once in his or her lifetime
Kaaba	the House of Allah in Makkah, originally built by Prophets Abraham and Ishmael
Ramadan	the ninth month in the Islamic calendar; the month of obligatory fasting
shahadah	the Islamic testimony of faith: *Ash-hadu al-la ilaha illa Allah, wa ash-hadu anna Muhammadan Abduhu wa Rasooluhu.* (I testify that there is no deity worthy of worship except Allah, and I testify that Muhammad is His slave and messenger.)
taghoot	idols; everything evil that is worshipped

1 If a word has become part of the English language (i.e., is found in a dictionary of Standard English), that spelling is used in this book.

www.ingramcontent.com/pod-product-compliance
Ingram Content Group UK Ltd.
Pitfield, Milton Keynes, MK11 3LW, UK
UKHW021359190726
13845UKWH00028B/774

9 788119 946433